a banner year.

appelquist

a banner year.

poems:
iris appelquist

EMP
Kansas City, Missouri
www.empbooks.com

Copyright 2017 by Iris Appelquist

All rights reserved. No part of this book may be reproduced, scanned, or distributed in any printed or electronic form, including information storage and retrieval systems, without permission. Please do not participate in or encourage piracy of copyrighted materials in violation of the author's rights. Please purchase only authorized editions.

First Edition: 11 7 5 3 2 1
ISBN: 978-0-9985077-8-1

This book is a work of fiction. Names, characters, places, dates, and incidents are products of the author's imagination, or are used fictitiously, satirically, or as parody. Any resemblance to actual persons, living or dead, business establishments, events, or locales is entirely coincidental.

Layout & Design: Jeanette Powers

table of contents

the agreement
september
october
november
may
winter
march
june
july
shadow
january
february
december
august
april
a banner year

the agreement

we don't know   what is a day
the depth   of its eyes   or width of its reach
the limit it seeks to expose   all odds in gaining
an open palmed gesture   a reception   a request
the answer the   solution
resolve
is only   yes   yes
in the language of   cells and DNA the   language they
use to   communicate with time
besides us   as a product   a result
us having to do   the damned and
insipid
measuring   of everything   and our course
through it   yes   in the
signals and signs   that the earth uses
that computers use   yes   and the
tragic   please
the ringing ardor   of a beg   looming
the bow of each   dusk you are not
done now   or ever

september

i can't go back and   make you live like
you should have   up to and forward
we can't go back   and get yours either
it is how it was   always resistant to
deviance and here i am   flinching at the wind
fantasizing your eulogy   in which
i say the right thing   instead of the nice
thing we can't begin   again   we can never
go back home   i wish i would have
broken open the vault   of our failures
a long time ago except   it is how it was
there is a lock   on the door
i try to picture it   try to imagine taking
the pins   out of the hinges.

october

except it is how it was　　the door opens in　　and i
　　can hear singing　　in there　　the key is a ray
　　　　　　that pierces through　　except
　　　　　　　　　the winter wars　　as
　　　　　　　shadow does　　and the winter
　　　　　　　no longer yields　　we all are
　　　　　　　　　called to cede　　some
　　　　　　　　　　pieces and parts of
　　　　　　　　　　our power　　like
　　　　　　　　　　a lost ray　　cut off
　　　　　　　　from the lock　　the door
　　　　　　　opens in　　i try to imagine
　　　　　　　　　　taking the pins
　　　　　　　　from the hinges　　and
　　　　　　　leaving the door　　hung
　　　　　　　　　limp　　from a locked
　　　　　　　socket　　except　　it is
　　　　　　　　　　　how it was

november

there is a place i live   that i don't actually
live in   it is a home to hide my
hoard of impossible futures   and the kitsch
of my failure

it's where my daughter's   father's arrears are
sent   and where the   meaning
of support arrives in the form of   dollars
my daughter is beginning   to move herself in there
too

the place i do and   do not live
in itself   is living it   attends and evolves
along with me   its bones are bowed
with decades of standing   and it is demanding
repair

when i was younger   i could still see the walls
and tried to hang there   a portrait of my mother   but
the place where   i live and do not live   spit out
the nail and her framed image   melted into the
floor

                  i feel the place   where i do and do not
        live   even when i am not there   i smell it
its corners project   themselves into other   spaces
           with a regular randomness   that i may never
                                                          learn

            the place where   i live and do not   live
       has taken things from me and   hidden them
i never stop finding   new rooms in which is   everything
                                           i cannot remember

              i feel i need to move   and i do   over
                   and over   sixteen times in ten years
              what i don't know   i don't know somehow
       eking out what i do   know that i don't   know
                there is no map   of this place where i
                live and do not live   it follows   me

          now there is only enough   space for my person
to stand amid the   horde just inside the   open door
           my daughter displaces things   and she suggests
                     building an addition   maybe
                                  an outbuilding.

             the place where i   live and do not   live

groans   whenever i pull a matchbook
from my pocket   and breathes
the flame from my fingers   wooden matches
pour through the gutters   there it rains
every day   i'm teaching my daughter   to play
with fire   i know that it will be   our only
way.

may

        we exceptions do take   to
leave out   lay waste   sate
the base   forget to sleep and
remember president's day
we fuck each other through
holes in our wallets   and will
fail to escape   fail to feel the
chains   fail to see   fail to
be.

we exceptions do take
and glory it   abide the shadow
sneak the sun   placeless and
burning too   we keep reaching
for a phantom member   some
kind of neither-region
utility   as dreams are
inductive.

we exceptions do take
truth   but are immune to its

curative effect   a force of
confound   for what is called
the greater good   getting angry
doesn't help   it's mutual   the
shadow   the winter
we have destroyed
ourselves in the future

  winter

        wouldn't we   love   an answer or
    salve   wouldn't we   welcome the
                solution   to our searching

                                wouldn't we   love to
                            not have to   question.

                                            to just not.

march

the shadow winter   the winter
that operates in secret   the shadow
winter seizes shards   of tulip
the burgeoning green   hazarded
in an old spiritual

about surrender   to the plan
god has   we must reject the
impulse to die   as frequently as
we indulge the impulse to thrive

it is a wet paper bag   which we
are trying to dry   as long as
we live   fingering wants creep
the light   i glint sideways
in the window   the wraith of me
close and dense   closer and
denser it moves   to supplant
me in the mirror   and the
idiot pink peach tree   flounders
in the strafe   our shadow

winter stalks   the stems of shrub roses
rations the light   we fight to
describe   not the absence of
hope but   the absence of the
possibility of hope   and
gradations of perfection   against
the opposite of perfection

don't be obtuse   it's the zeitgeist
stupid   the penultimate
darkest dark upon which   the
dawn is predicated   our
shadow winter waxes   still

june

where a vacation won't fit   i can always put
the last of my grass   a moment   of quiet repose
because   my getting older   and getting wiser
is no longer   a requirement   nor a reasonably
likely outcome.

maybe my fear   of language sits in
the same   bath that Electra took   or Sappho
when i linger   amid the chaff   bound
to get bit   things have reasons
you know.

when the sun   screaming   rose and did not
stop   we saw daytime a lot   different we
cling   now   to winter   and long for rain
even as we   drown   drowsy with lust
and its own   special   grief.

july

it's the light and the weight
hanging together like that
clearly making a bed as if it wasn't
my own hands moving things
clanging against my body against
time and the things time
takes from me from us.
we were there when
we were us being us there
we were just making a
scene.
broken open i land in
an odd place where nothing
meant the things they mean
meaning words were many
things besides themselves
while also being
themselves. the sun
flares and my heart
under it racing broken
open my body wants to
sing.

shadow

at sixty-eight   miles per hour
someone   has to explain   to me
the difference   between an orchid
and   a penis

i cannot assign meaning   to either
thing   besides fragility   i can't see
very far   in front of me

at seventy-two   miles per hour
a commonly held   belief
further entrenches   itself

its absurdity   echoes back
its   absurdity echoes   back its
absurdity echoes   it's absurd   it's

at   eighty-six   miles per hour
there is blood   on the road
in the water   and

we drink   too much   we don't see
very far   in front of us

        at zero   miles   per hour
a complicated metaphor   stakes out
    its perfect form   on the side of
            the road

    someone   has to explain to me
    the difference   between then
        and   then.

january

we all know already   and build
our barricades against   reality with a fluent
hand our bodies   rigid with resistance   creating other
smaller   escapable situations   we all
know already so   dull the fact   that where
we meet is not a plane or place   it is a vector
unresponsive to the influence   of external forces
wheeling wheedling   pretending to not know
already as we do   purpose is predicated   on ignorance
the willful neglect   by which we are permitted
to make comparisons   at all   creating other
denser shadows   by which we define summer   with which
we illustrate our desire   to unknow

february

i was ready to   show myself
a beginning   infant collisions
with the fourth dimension   the warm
green against the   limpid
shadow against   the tyrant winter
we are   yet   recovered.

made whole we still   thieve
we beg and borrow   we
create opportunities   for others
to make themselves
available   we show
ourselves   and ask to also   see.

this place was born   between
layers   of operation   we
cannot   normally   attend
passed down   to us
in a formless   parcel
we cannot conserve   there
should be   something
that makes us   feel like a
kid again.

december

december twenty-fifth   at the zenith of utility
an apex   that describes the point
at which we   become fused
     with vector and vehicle
a triad in opposition
to all other forces in motion
plotted with   a measure
of operation tongues and
hands do not speak
     the action is merely   implied
remembering the axis   with
searching cries
that whimper   sometimes scream
sometimes breathe   standing
outside   in your shirtsleeves
     on Christmas morning
at the outskirts of   our known world
the grass   green
the sun   shining   hungry

august

not in the mood   to talk about anything
as if   anything   was gonna
get talked out   but whatever
it's just the way   how it happens   the intent
is there opportunity   too it's just that
i don't   understand it

it turns out i have   too much faith
in the vehicles   moving feeling   to words
and out   and being

being made   and real
out there   just way   out there
out front   an eternal experiment   at evolution
of the spirit the   nature of approach or
getting clear of all the   shit   the shit
that makes its home   behind the eyes
and the shit   flying always

not in the mood   to take it off of
you   please   just give it
to me i'm   in there already   waiting

see i know things that   you don't know i know
things you don't know   you don't know   it's like
that   it is how it was
always

turns out   we have
a lot   in common
but you can't   play peekaboo
with your damn   self
after all   it doesn't super
work   that way

but alright   ok

april

a voice i hear   from my seat on the porch
     it echoes the high end   reaches me
unimpeded   it is a stretch   starts low
     ends up in a wail   i cannot say

     whether it is a cat   getting
mauled or   a baby   dropped
on the sidewalk   the lurching
and plaintive sound
of it   i can't tell

a banner year

the sun will come out tomorrow   bet your bottom dollar
    and that five gallons of gas   are gonna last a
whole week
a whole winter   a whole war   a holy war
    is a just war   is a shadow war
making the world   safe for winning

the public domain
    is pitching us forward   we are lunging toward
a new paradigm   dark in its stricture
    its scripture is a living
document   growing with no   feeding on
no nourished by our   unceasing pain

playing the game   can't change a
    fucking thing
the grief theater   now accessory to the
    ensemble of
guilt   he among you without sin   may cast the first stone
rome wasn't built   in a day   the clock is ticking
    sorry we're closed   thanks
we're open

coping is hard the knowing of facts and
we are pitted against ourselves
each other the division so stark
in its presentation its effect perfect
against the void

you don't know what you don't know
and you can't know what you didn't know
until you knew it fast fictions calculate
their fall and we give our children warnings instead
of
hope.

also by iris appelquist

NICE FEELINGS
where we were we were there
BRIAR
blunt trauma

irisappelquist@gmail.com

www.ingramcontent.com/pod-product-compliance
Lightning Source LLC
Chambersburg PA
CBHW020627300426
44113CB00007B/795